This edition published by Parragon Books Ltd in 2016
and distributed by

Parragon Inc.
440 Park Avenue South, 13th Floor
New York, NY 10016
www.parragon.com

ISBN 978-1-4748-5116-9

Printed in China

In today's hectic world, life moves pretty fast, and it can be tricky to find time to chill out. Sometimes it can seem like you have to become a super hero just to keep up with everything that needs to be done each day!

But we should try to take some time out on a regular basis, and what better way to escape the real world than with a DC Super Heroes coloring book? It checks off all the right boxes, with the added bonus of producing something awesome in the process.

There's no special skill or equipment required; just choose a page featuring your favorite DC Super Heroes and begin bringing the characters to life with color.

Just as the DC Super Heroes have skills ready to be revealed when the time is right, we all have an inner artist waiting to be set free. And like Superman, Batman, and The Flash, there are no limits to what you can achieve!

So it's time to aim high, be strong, and use your laser vision to complete each page of *Comic Art Coloring*. And most of all . . . have fun!

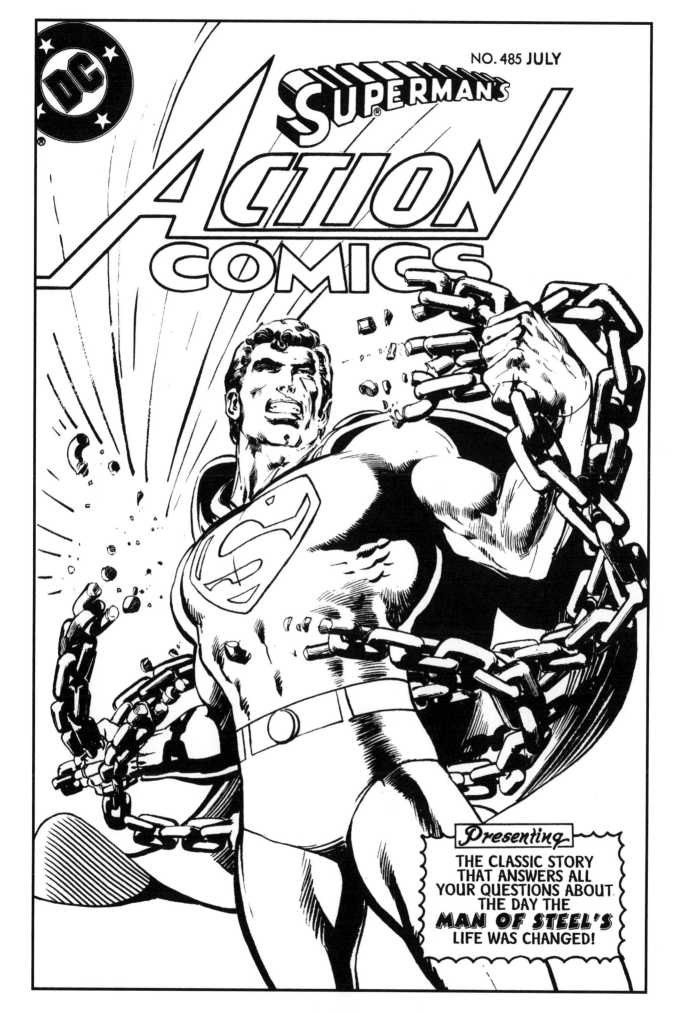

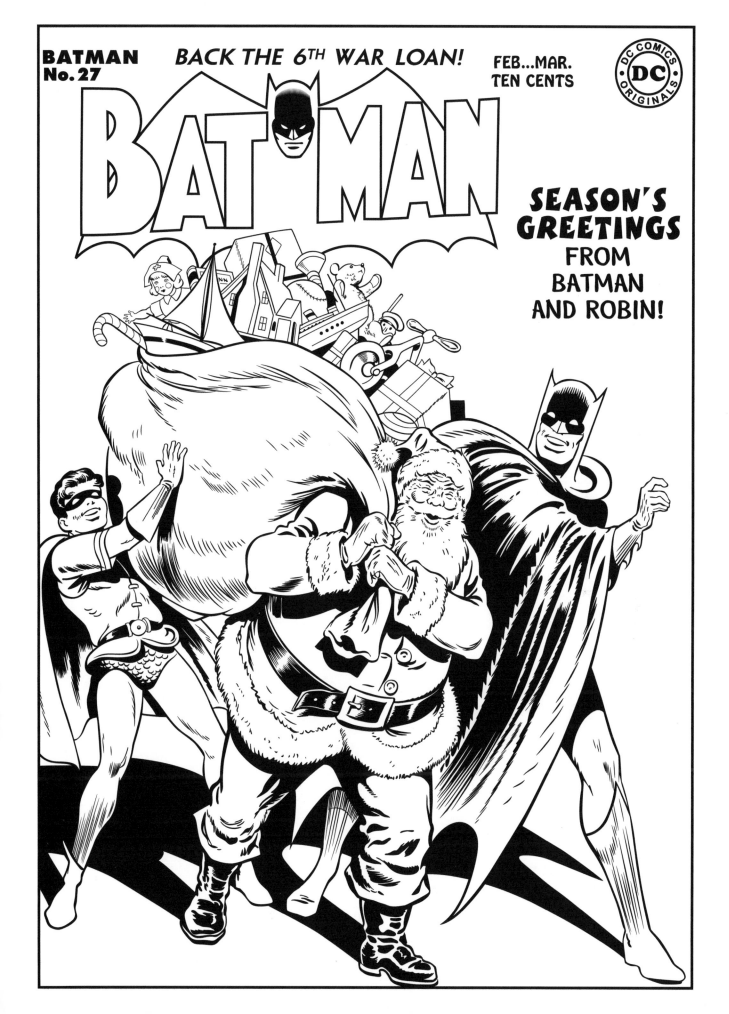

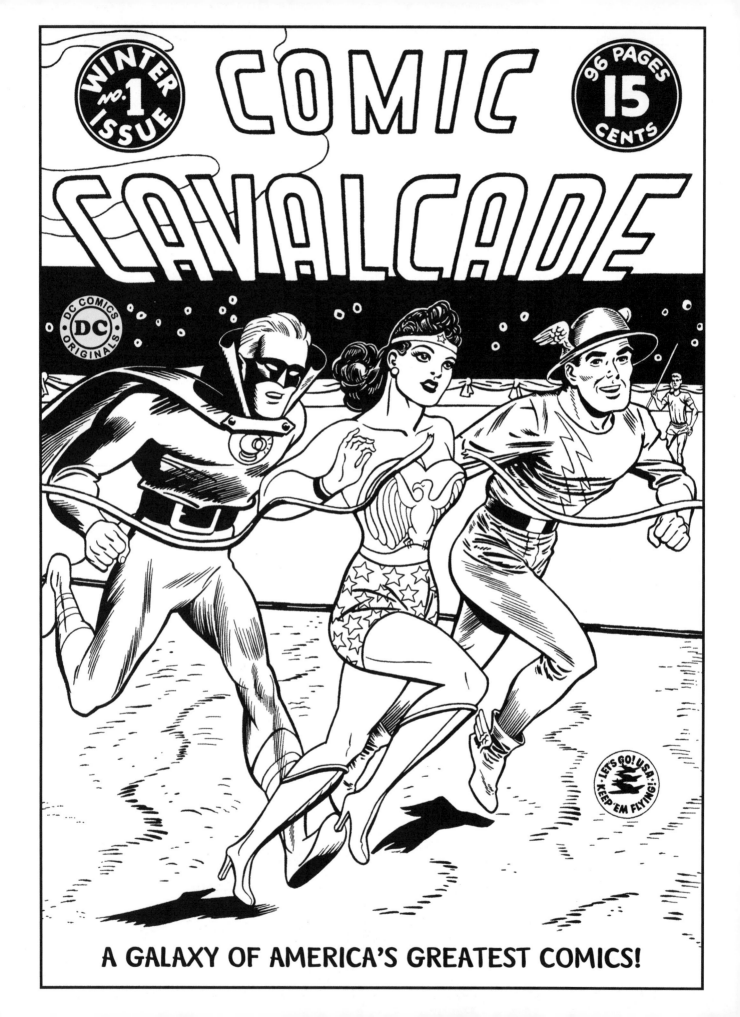

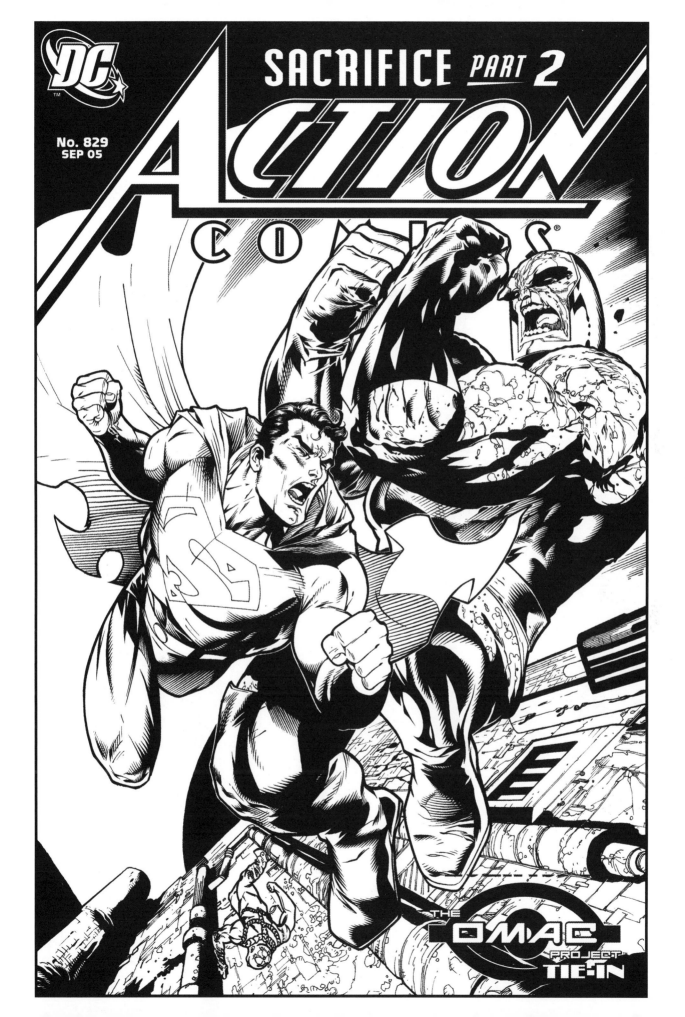

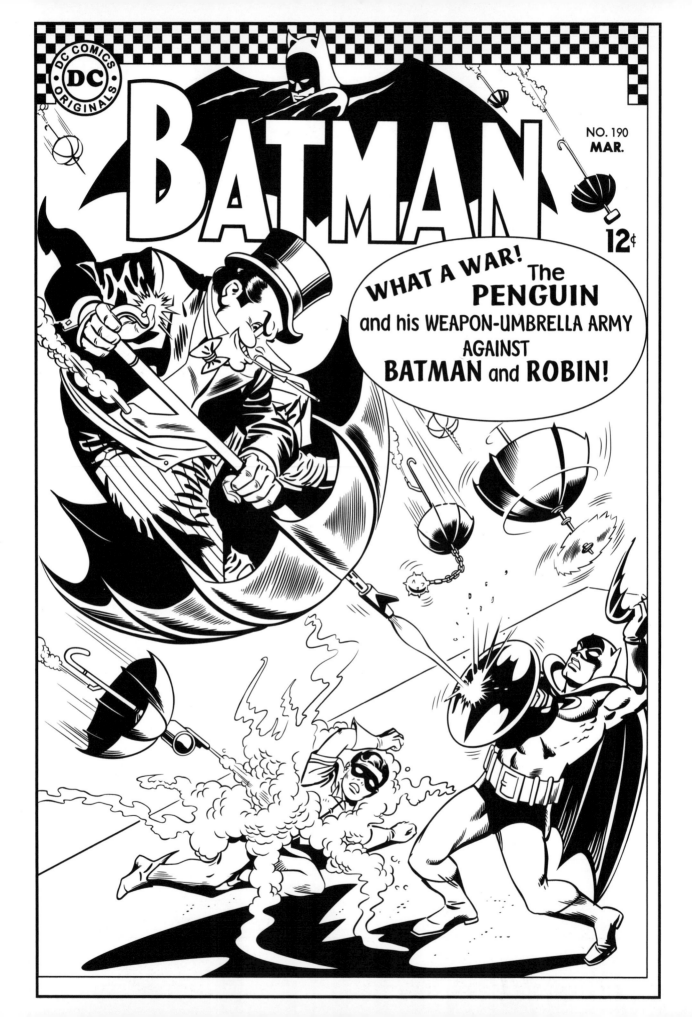

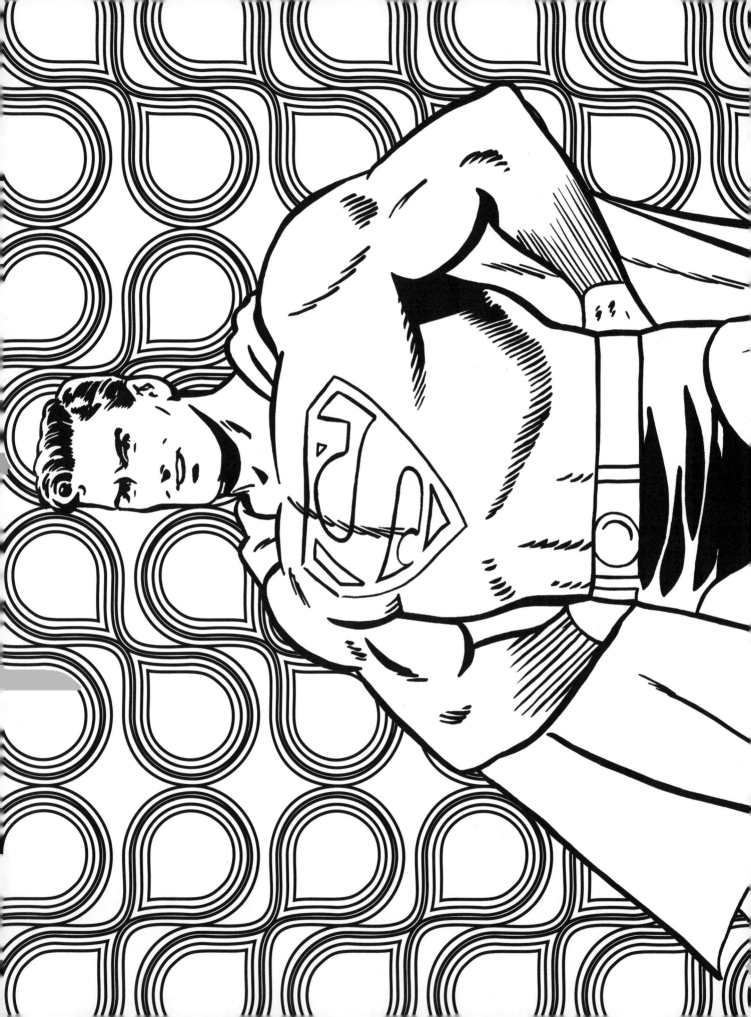

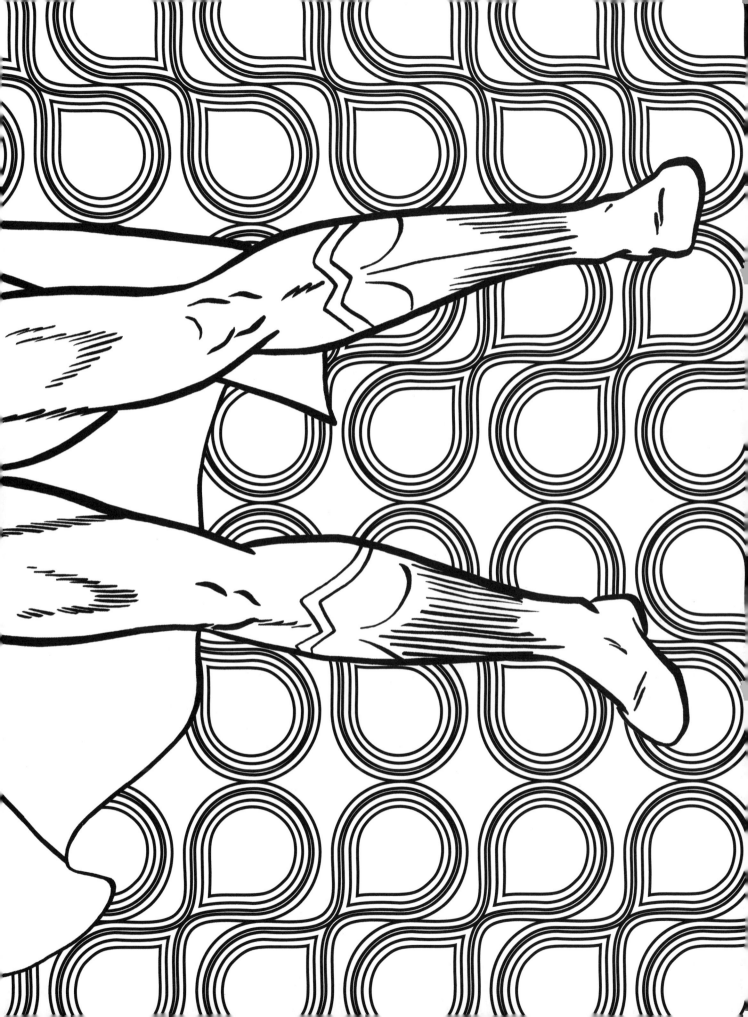

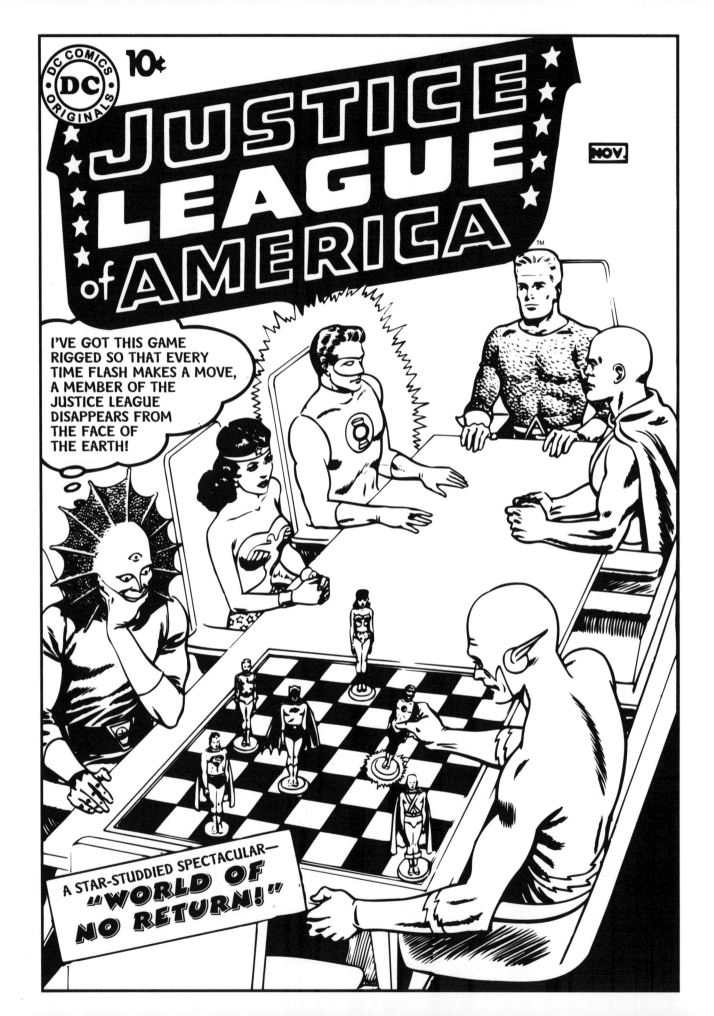

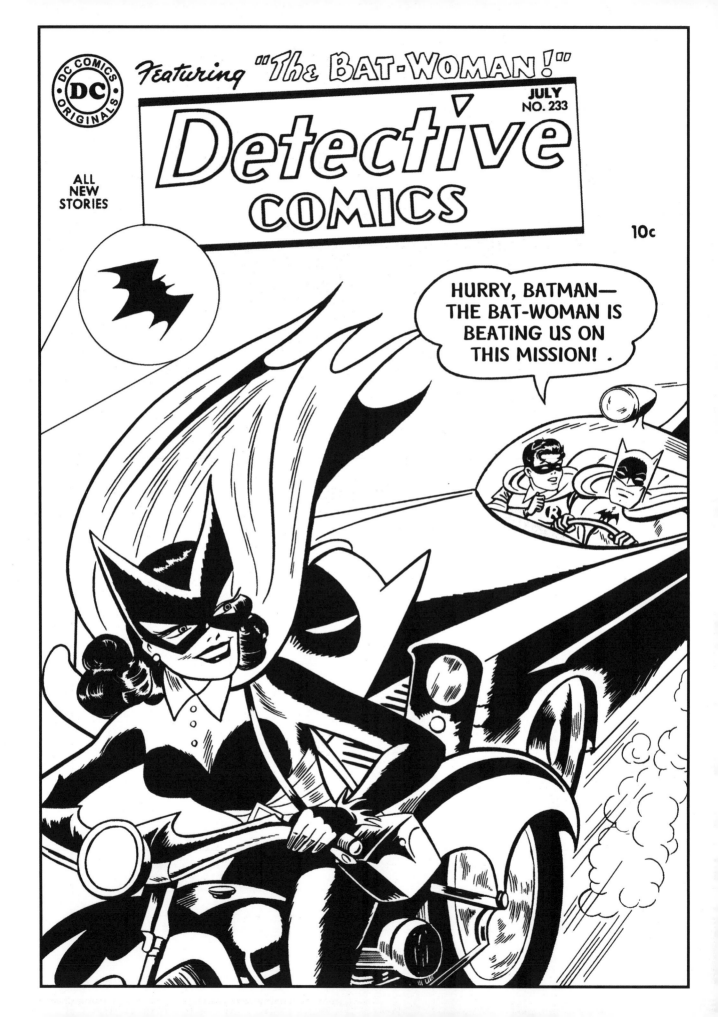

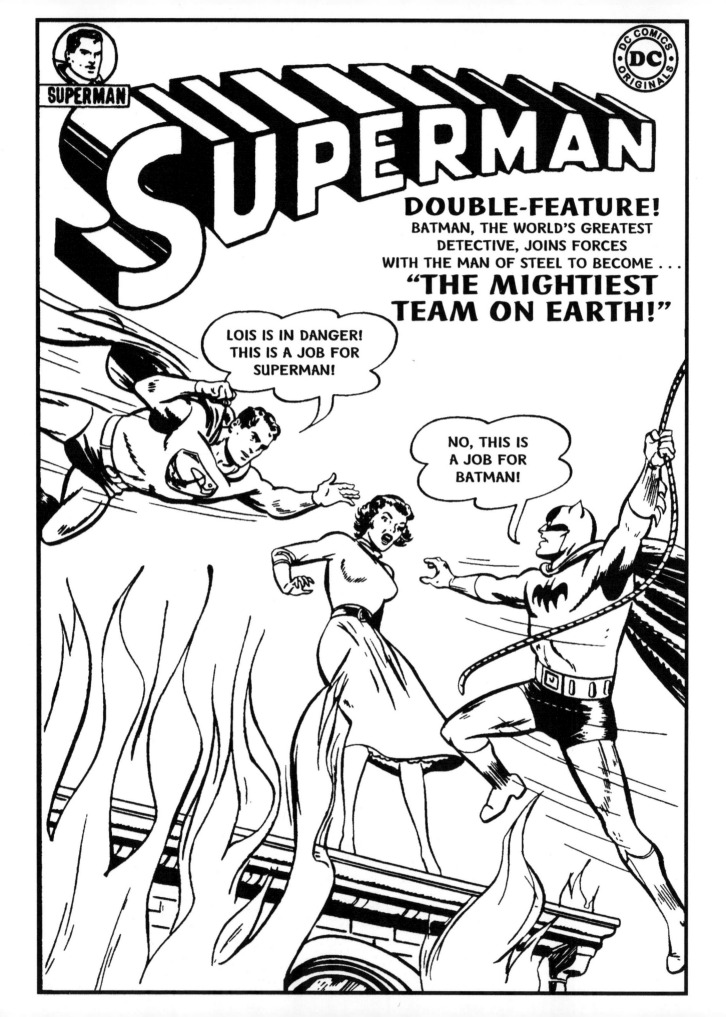

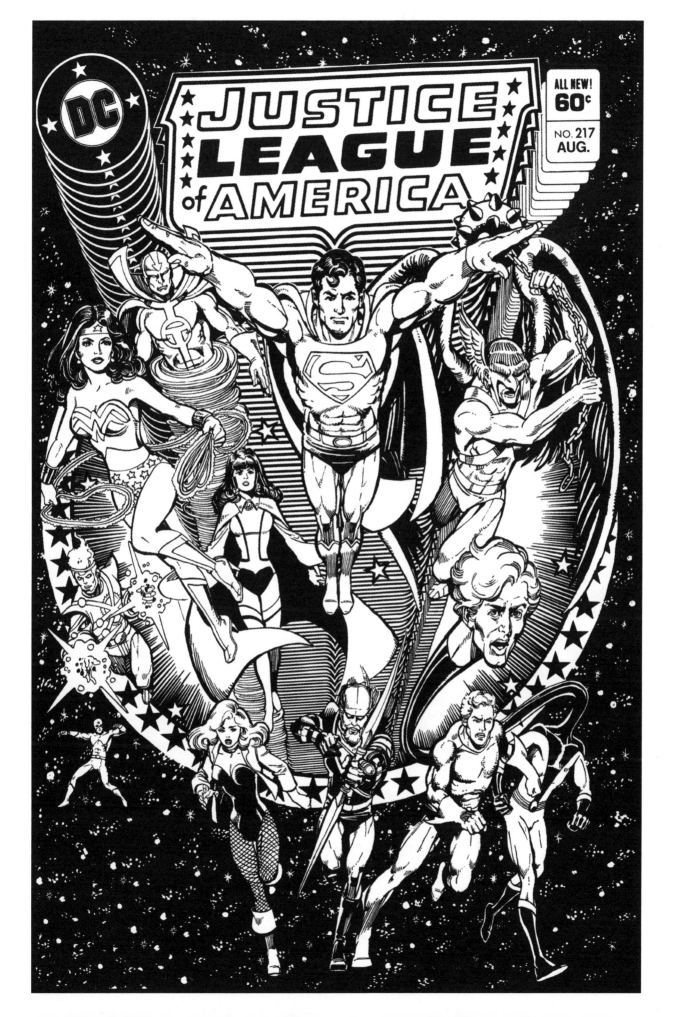

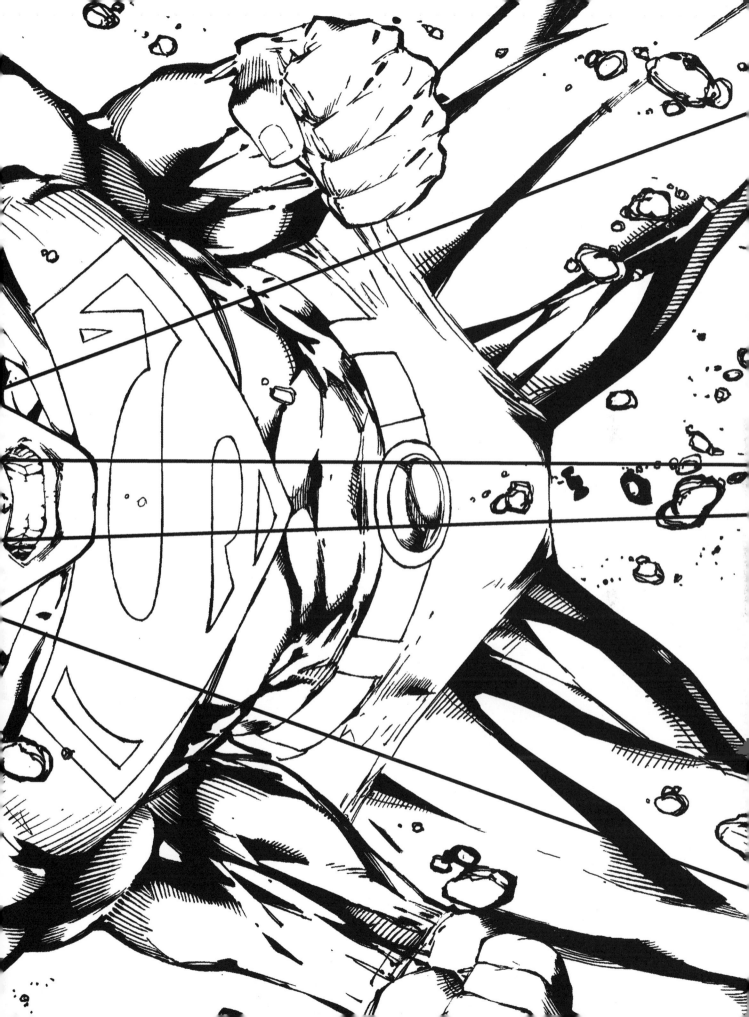

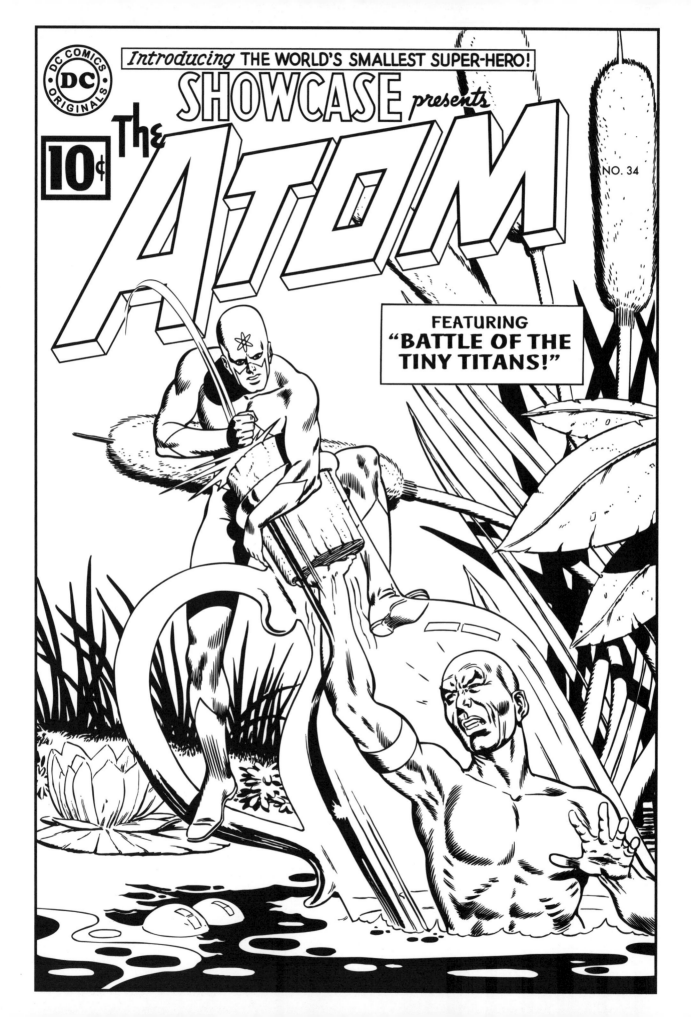

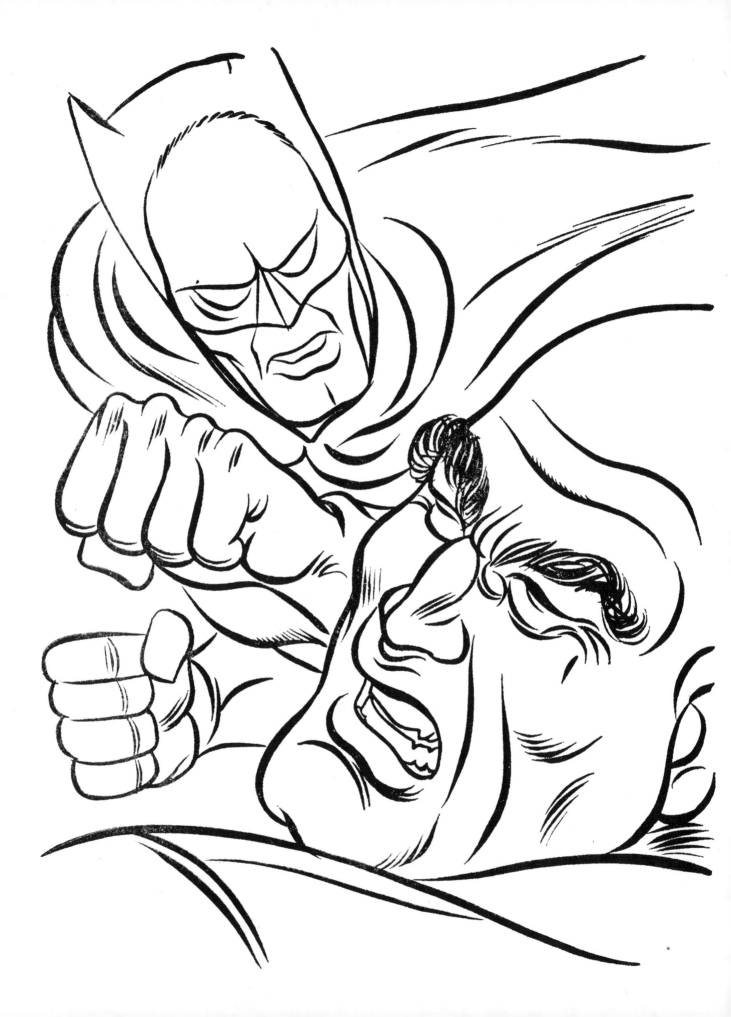

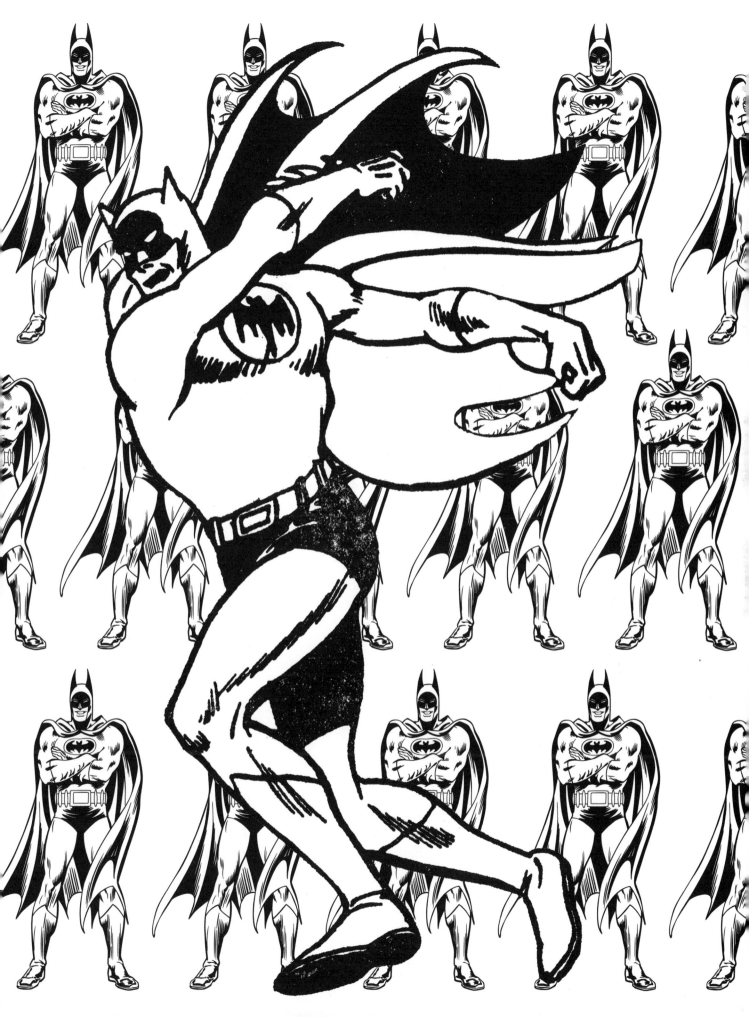

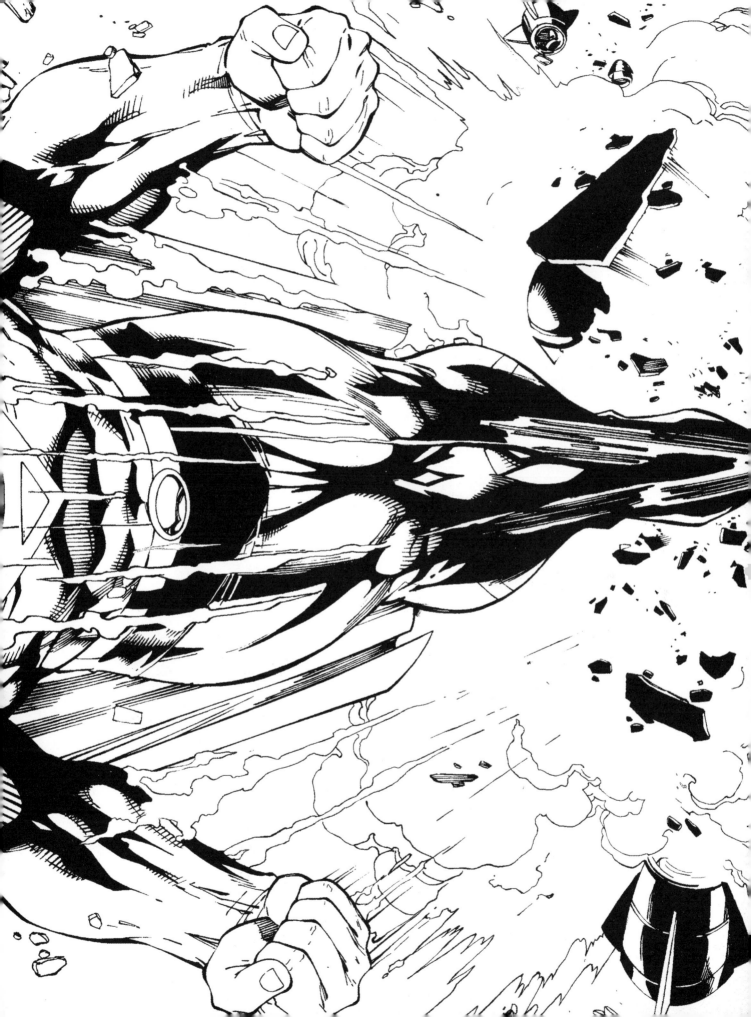

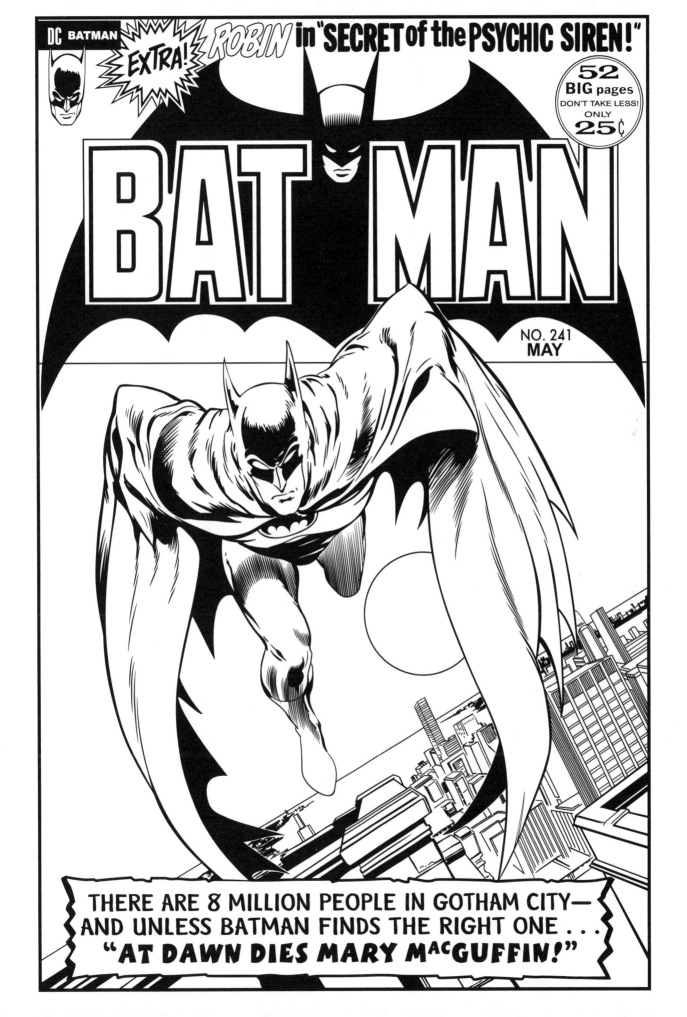

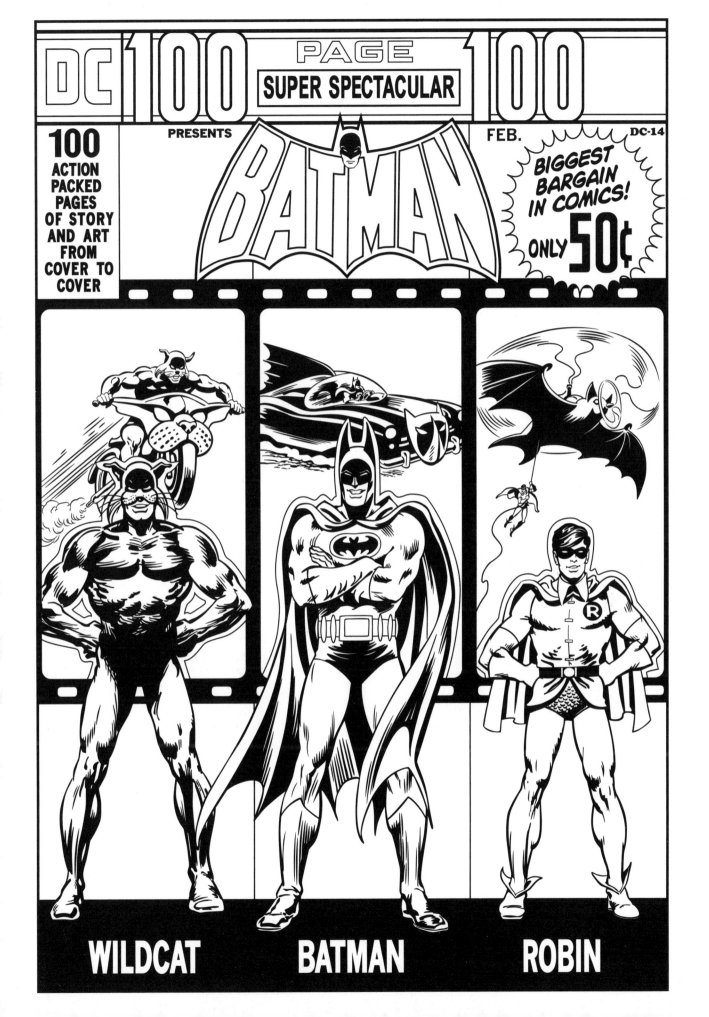